What's the difference that makes the difference?

Your guide to small business branding:
a workbook from The Branding Workshop

Yvonne Fuchs & Sue Alouche

www.thebrandingworkshop.com

also by Yvonne Fuchs:
The Art of Knowing Yourself

ISBN 978-1-4478-3840-1

Our grateful thanks go to all the clients who have undertaken the branding workshop during the last 15 years, from whom we have learnt so much.

Acknowledging that we all stand on the shoulders of those who went before, we thank those who have inspired us in business and creativity, by their example, research and inspiration.

To our initial editor James Woolway, thank you for getting us started and to Sharon Adams our final editor, for shaping, developing and editing with such clarity and dedication.

Contents ●●●

Introduction ●●●

When the economic climate is tough, some companies survive, and some don't. What differentiates those that succeed is something that goes beyond the price and quality of their product or service.

Whether you intend it or not, your business has a unique set of qualities that define it in the minds of your customers. This is the essence of your brand, and it is these qualities that determine how clients feel about spending money with you. You might be perceived as ethical, convenient, useful, dated, cheap, cutting-edge, aspirational. The list goes on, but how well would your customers' descriptions match your own ideas about your business?

Strong branding builds a strong business. Whether you own a local café, or an international fashion label, the brand is what drives customer loyalty and is therefore the most important asset your business can have.

What makes a small brand-led business successful is YOU. Your beliefs, what you understand about yourself and how you operate, all influence the success of your business. The aim of this book is to help you capture this essential information and translate it into a brand. This is how all businesses become truly successful.

In the 10 years we have been running The Branding Workshop we have been greatly inspired by the clients we have worked with. Many of them had no idea that what really made the difference to how they ran their businesses (and made them successful) was themselves.

In other words: the difference that makes the difference is YOU!

How does this book work?

This book will take you through the stages in the Branding Workshop process, as shown in the chart below. In each section, you'll see which stage of the journey you're at, then complete exercises and tasks to reach the relevant goals.

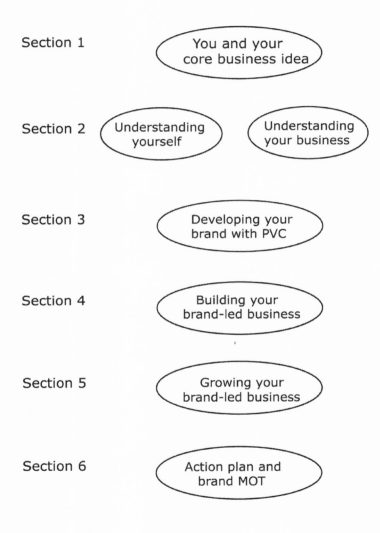

This is a practical manual, so we will be asking you to put some effort into developing your brand. You didn't think we would do it all for you, did you? We assure you it will be fun, but a few ground rules are important.

 Throughout the book, you will find **exercises** marked with this icon. These form the core of the Branding Workshop process. Use the space provided for your answers, or feel free to use extra paper if you wish. This information will help you consolidate what you learn about yourself, and we will be referring back to your answers as we progress.

 You will find **examples** denoted by this icon. Here, we suggest real business versions of the ideas we're talking about, bringing the theory to life.

 Finally, you will find **walk-the-talk tips**, marked with this icon. Be sure to make use of these, as they are the key to translating your new-found knowledge into business results.

It's very useful to share the exercises with colleagues and friends who can give their perspective on you and your business. As you complete the exercises and try out the tips, this book will evolve into the basis of a branding handbook for your individual business.

We try to avoid jargon, but if any of the terms we've used are unfamiliar, the **Glossary** on page 132 will explain them.

The **Resources** Section on page 134 will guide you towards further information.

About the Authors

Yvonne Fuchs, founder of the award-winning Branding Workshop, UK and Sue Alouche owner, Créativité Consultants, France. Yvonne and Sue have worked together on many projects in recent years.

Having studied branding models developed by the world's top agencies, such as Interbrand, Landor and Corporate Edge, we realised there was an opportunity to simplify their strategies and make them accessible and workable for small businesses. While they looked at the attributes of corporate structures, our task was to look at the individuals behind small businesses.

Yvonne Fuchs has been involved in the business world for over 30 years and has been coaching and mentoring businesses for over a decade in the areas of branding, marketing and business development. An NLP Master, Yvonne is passionate about empowering her small business clients to become successful, irrespective of their starting point. Her ability to inspire others through creativity and business coaching has been her unique contribution to the SME world.

Using her insight and experience to encourage change and entrepreneurship, Yvonne has worked within both her own creative businesses and her family manufacturing business. She has held several senior posts in education and commerce, and has won a number of awards including the One to One Best for Business award (2000) for her original work on Branding, and the Business Link Spirit of Enterprise award (2007). Her current business has been described as a milestone in making a complex business tool accessible to SMEs, independents and the not-for-profit sector.

As well as an MA in Design Studies from Central St Martins, London Yvonne holds the award of Consultant Practitioner from NLPU and has numerous coaching qualifications at her disposal.

Sue Alouche has worked in the Design Industry for 28 years in both the UK, and for the last 7 years, in France. Sue started her career working in leading UK design agencies such as Conran Associates, The Design Solution (as Associate Director). Sue worked at Reich & Petch of Canada and also ran her own design consultancy for 5 years. She is now a workshop facilitator, visiting lecturer and independent consultant in the domains of branding, creativity and future thinking. She works for the best private continuing education establishments (Grand Ecoles) in France, such as Audencia Management School and l'Ecole de Design Nantes Atlantique.

Sue was commissioned by Yvonne Fuchs to develop the creative brand strategies resulting from the Branding Workshop's principles. Over a period of 7 years she worked with both SMEs and entrepreneurs and won a Rubican Award for her creative direction. Her belief in the efficiency and creativity of the Branding Workshop led her to take The Branding Workshop to France in 2009.

Sue received an MA in Design Studies from Central School of Art and Design, London in 1997, specialising in Aroma Design for visually impaired people. Together with Dr Geoff Crook, her course Director, she formed the basis of the first sensory design laboratory in the UK.

Last year Sue received the "Observeur du Design 2010" for her strategic teamwork on brand positioning for Bluering - an innovative new concept in dry dock marinas in France.

Section 1: Background ●●●

You and your
core business idea

Understanding
yourself

Understanding
your business

Developing your
brand with PVC

Building your
brand-led business

Growing your
brand-led business

Action plan and
brand MOT

You and your core business idea

Owning a business is a wonderful way to express who you are and make a living. Some of the largest brands like Coca Cola or Levis came from a small business person having an idea and taking it forward. But the key to being successful in business is to be very business-like. This means think clearly, focus on the results you want and learn from others' experience.

In this book we are going to share with you our knowledge of having worked with small and growing businesses over many years. We believe that if you follow our suggestions in this book you'll have a very solid basis from which to grow your business.

Although this book is meant for businesses who have developed a product or service and know where they're going to sell it and at what price, you will gain a great deal from this process if you are still developing your idea, and whether you are trading yet or not.

What is a Brand?

It's not just about logos...

We know from experience that owners of small businesses are often confused about the term 'brand', and rightly so. Isn't branding something big businesses obsess over and spend fortunes on?

The dictionary definition of a brand is a 'trademark or distinctive name identifying a product or a manufacturer', but a great brand is much more than just that. Every business, no matter how small, has a brand. The question is whether these brands have been created intentionally or accidentally. It is essential to know if your brand is actually communicating what you are really all about.

Conscious Branding

There is no doubt in our minds that small businesses which deliberately develop a strong brand presence are far more likely to succeed. This means much more than a snappy trading name, strapline, typefaces, colours or logos. It is everything that a business does and has done - its biography - and most importantly, if you are the founder of your business, these things are a communication of YOU.

We can think of the brand in terms of DNA, a hidden presence or essence which is at the heart of all that you do. Your brand DNA is defined by multiple strands, and these will reflect many things including your life experiences, who you are, what your customers think of you, what your employees say and what the media reports. So the question is: if you knew that in every action your business took you were in the process of creating your brand, would that change how you do business?

In a world of social media, we not only have to develop our brand but also to manage its communication and the brand's ongoing position in the marketplace. We will look at specific methods and strategies for this later on.

Standing out from the crowd

You know that no two people are alike, even twins have their differences. The same applies to businesses. For your business to be successful, whether it's you as a freelance designer, a creative business, a retailer, a food producer - you have to stand out from the crowd.

"In a world where products and services in most sectors can be imitated virtually overnight by competitors you need to present yourself differently"

Peter, Drucker, Harvard Business School

The good news is that branding is a strategy that helps you do this very effectively. It is such a powerful mechanism in business that the world around you is full of brands competing for your attention.

A brand is a way of expressing what is uniquely YOU. It will empower you to shine your light out there. It will give you competitive advantage. It will give your business added value. It will set you apart.

At the early stages of a business, you and your business are pretty synonymous. Your beliefs, values and personality are very much those of your business. As a business grows, the real trick is to keep what inspired you in the first place embedded in the culture and brand of the ongoing business.

A good example of this is Anita Roddick, founder of The Body Shop. Her attitudes, personality and vision were what made it such a great brand. She started off very small but was able to keep her vision intact as the business grew, and it will greatly help your success if you can also maintain your vision as your business grows.

 There are many high-profile businesses today in which the personality of the owner shines through. Think of Jamie Oliver, driven by his passion that good food should be available to all. This led him to set up Fifteen, a restaurant and training centre for young employed people, as well as tackling school dinners at government and street level. Quite diverse activities, but all aligned with his core belief in helping people enjoy fresh food.

How Branding works

A tattoo in the mind

Do you have a tattoo? If so, you probably had it done for a good reason, as something to mark you out, or to be remembered by? If you don't have one, you perhaps know someone who has and why they got it. If not, you could ask a friend who does. It will be interesting to understand why that individual chose to mark themselves out.

Why is branding so powerful as a business development tool? Branding is all about creating something memorable in the mind of the customer, an indelible impression of what the brand is about: a tattoo in the mind of clients and potential clients.

 List some brands which have built tattoos in your mind and which you admire:

eg Howies, Apple, your local café...

Symbols and Rituals in Branding

As the marketplace becomes more and more crowded, simple powerful symbols are taking over. Apple's trash can, and the greetings "smiley" when the computer is turned on are two that instantly spring to mind. Every single Apple icon passes the ultimate test of being singularly associated with Apple, even when they stand alone.

A new breed of brands has grown up around daily rituals and activities that were unknown a few years ago: "Googling" and "Tweeting" as well as new meanings for familiar terms like "Watching" "Liking" and "Sharing".

The way these brands are experienced, with their distinctively formatted and predictable nature makes them compelling, maybe even addictive. These are international brand examples, but do you have opportunities for developing long-lasting symbols or rituals associated with your brand? What symbols might they be?

 In the US, people have been paid to have brand names, logos and web addresses tattooed onto their bodies. Casino promotions and restaurants offering free lunches for life are among the better-known examples. We're not suggesting you go this far, but these demonstrate the power a brand has to enter the psyche of a person.

We've seen that a brand is a set of attributes both tangible and intangible which exist in the mind of the customer. These are built up over time by using and experiencing the brand. We can therefore see that a brand is not just about logos, it is a collection of perceptions in the mind of the customer. This definition makes it absolutely clear that a brand is very different from a product or service.

From our perspective, when you build a brand you are aiming to pull your prospective customers towards you, but in order to do this you also have to push out the correct marketing messages. This is a bit like Dr Doolittle's creature the Pushmepullyou.

Marketing activity is all "Push". The way that customers are "pulled" towards you is by using branding to create a desire in them to come and find your product or service. So branding is like a magnet drawing clients towards you. In order to create the perceptions that you want your customers to have about your brand, you have to do some deep thinking about what YOU are about. We give you an exercise about Brand Rituals on page 76.

You'll need to consider what your core idea is and what your vision is for your brand. What promises will you make to your customers about what they can expect from you? How will you communicate to your customers that the way you do things is different from others. How do you express your uniqueness through your personality, your values and your culture?

Why do big businesses spend so much on their branding strategy? What do they know that others don't? We are here to let you in on a big secret... any business can develop a powerful brand. It doesn't matter how big or small your business is.

There are different types of brand images; some are seen as contemporary and cool, such as Converse and The Guardian. There are those that seem almost timeless and we presume they will always be around, such as the BBC or Dior. Perhaps their sheer commercial power, the strength of their product and pricing strategies enable them to ride out a recession. Coca-Cola and Tesco may be good examples here. Then we have innovative brands, such as Green & Blacks and the Co-op, who have championed Fairtrade products and ethical banking. These are companies that listen to their customers to create a whole new brand experience.

Then, there are those tired brands, who are just there when you walk past, hardly noticing them. The High Street is littered with unimaginative shops which do not deliver a great brand experience and as a result risk being left behind. You can think of a couple in your local area, can't you?

So which are you? Are you falling behind and ready for a makeover or do you want to ensure your brand is the best it can be and doing everything it can to further your business? Perhaps you have not yet developed your brand and want to ensure firm foundations are in place as you launch your business.

In all cases, the next part of this book will help you define who you are, where you are going, what you offer and how to flaunt it. It will tell you when to 'push' and when to 'pull', and, most important of all, how to survive in a very competitive marketplace.

Summary

In this section you've seen that:

- a brand is much more than a trademark
- a brand is the essential DNA of your business – the hidden strands that carry vital information
- a brand is a way of expressing what is uniquely YOU, helping your business to stand out from the crowd
- a brand is a collection of perceptions in the mind of customers
- branding is like a tattoo in the mind of clients and potential clients
- small businesses which deliberately develop a strong brand presence are far more likely to succeed

Now we can start to work on how to create a brand for you and your business idea.

Section 2: Getting to know YOU & your business ●●●

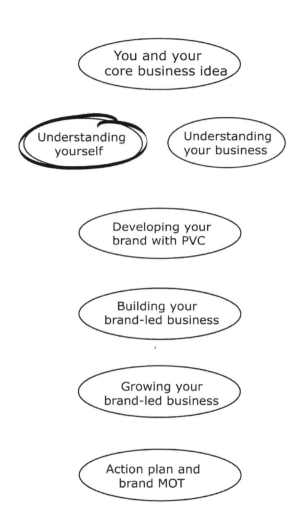

You and your core business idea

Understanding yourself

Understanding your business

Developing your brand with PVC

Building your brand-led business

Growing your brand-led business

Action plan and brand MOT

Who do you think you are?

In this section we will take you through a series of steps which will help you identify how aspects of your personality relate directly to qualities of your brand and therefore your business.

All brands start from small beginnings, from the vision of an individual entrepreneur. Often people start in business because of a personal passion. Perhaps they love art, helping others, cooking or creating something new and exciting. However, as we will come to see in this book, creating a successful brand is much more than just doing something really well.

Your brand is defined by the way that YOU do things, and that is a result of who YOU are and what YOU believe. It's not just about some clever marketing strategy being carried out by 'the professionals', it's something that means something to you.

So in the words of Steve Covey in his seminal work *7 Habits of Highly Effective People* let's "start with the end in mind".

What's your vision for your business?

If you don't have a clear idea, picture or desire for what you want your business to become, it is unlikely that you will achieve anything!

The lifestyle you want your business to give you is also really important, many people start businesses in order to change the way they currently work. They might want more time with their family. They might want to create something new. Let us see how to get in touch with these desires.

 Henry Ford had the core vision to bring individual transport to all people, he was able to visualise a future where the countryside and wide open spaces in America would be within the reach of ordinary people.

Your Future Life: as your first exercise, we want you to think about where it is you want to get to, your life goals. What you want your business to achieve for you personally.

In the space that follows, jot down thoughts that describe the successful you of the future. If you like to do things visually, you may like to create a collage from magazine pictures that express your vision.

Make it fun, and include any role models, exciting activities and beautiful locations. We will refer back to this later.

Consider the following:

- What does it look like?

- Who else is there?

- Think about sounds, tastes, smells.

- What's your experience of having this lifestyle?

- What's your ideal working day? Imagine your day in a magazine article – how would you describe it?

- Use the space below to draw, write, doodle or collage your ideas.

Now let's talk about your business in relation to your vision. For you to be successful in business, your business has to be able to deliver that lifestyle you have just created.

You and your core business idea

Understanding yourself

Understanding your business

Developing your brand with PVC

Building your brand-led business

Growing your brand-led business

Action plan and brand MOT

Create a set of goals for YOU and your business: state your answers in the positive, often we say what we don't want, *eg I don't want to struggle financially*, so try to change these negative statements into positive ones.

Here is an example, then it's your turn!

What goal do I want to achieve?	*I want a business that turns over 100k per year.*
What will that do for me?	*I will feel secure.*
How will I know when I'm there?	*I will have invoiced £100,000 worth of sales*
What will I be seeing, hearing and feeling when I've got it?	*I will be taking friends out to lunch, and will not be worried about the bill.*
What will I be saying to myself?	*I will be saying to myself well done you made it!*
What will I hear others saying about me?	*Look at what she has achieved with her vision and hard work.*
Can I get started on this goal and maintain this outcome?	*Yes, there is nothing stopping me, and it is so important that I will do what takes, so I will do less socialising and learn all I can.*
When do I want to achieve this by?	*In two years time.*
Where do I want to do this?	*Maybe from home initially, and eventually moving to France.*
With whom do I want to achieve it?	*By myself to begin with, and later with a business partner.*
Is there a positive quality of my current situation that I wish to preserve?	*I am currently working as part of a team in paid employment, and I want to retain that sense of team work in some way..*
Is this project worth the time and cost to me?	*Yes, I know I will have to put in a lot of extra time, but I will have the freedom to do things my way.*
Is this outcome in keeping with my sense of self and my values?	*Yes, I have always believed I have what it takes to be in business and I want to help others run their business successfully too.*

Now your version:

What goal do I want to achieve?	
What will that do for me?	
How will I know when I'm there?	
What will I be seeing, hearing and feeling when I've got it?	
What will I be saying to myself?	
What will I hear others saying about me?	
Can I get started on this goal and maintain this outcome?	
When do I want to achieve this by?	
Where do I want to do this?	
With whom do I want to achieve it?	
Is there a positive quality of my current situation that I wish to preserve?	
Is this project worth the time and cost to me?	
Is this outcome in keeping with my sense of self and my values?	

Know Yourself - Know your Business

You now have a vision of your future life and some ideas of how your business will deliver it. Now let's talk about YOU.

Business is not for the faint-hearted. If you want a successful business, much of how you build its brand will be based upon YOU! Therefore, it follows that you have to understand yourself in order to motivate yourself and inspire others. In doing this, you will begin to understand that YOU are at the core of your brand.

"to thine own self be true, And it must follow, as the night the day, Thou canst not then be false to any man"

Hamlet, William Shakespeare

The truth is that our personality is probably the most obvious thing about us. We know that people are subconsciously drawn towards certain types of people. We are often drawn to a person before we even consider their product. In order to develop your brand, your personality is key. So, you have to get to know yourself first.

Who Are You? We want you to describe yourself. What are the traits that make you YOU!

Are you Knowledgeable? Assertive? Vibrant? Creative? Dogged?

Give it some thought now and come up with the five words or phrases that sum you up. Test your answers on your friends, because they will know you best, or ask some friends to list their top five, then compare all the lists to identify your top answers.

List your top 5 personality traits:

1...

2...

3...

4...

5...

Use these aspects of your personality to form the experience that your customers receive when they engage with you and your brand. Your personality will give your brand a sense of being real, something that customers can relate to.

 Richard Branson is very much the figurehead of the Virgin empire brand and he has a vibrant, upbeat character. However, the most interesting thing about his personality when he was building his brand, was that whilst being to some extent a risk-taker he was also very media shy. These two traits made his brand personality more intriguing.

 Used well, blogs and social networks like Facebook and Twitter are great ways of developing and communicating your unique personality traits, but make sure your posts are consistent with your brand. How does your brand personality speak? If you say you are "serious" then you need to write in a serious way.

By using these sites you can build an on-line personality which really portrays the essence of who you are. A word of warning though: be careful what you talk about on-line in a casual way, one bad apple can spoil a whole barrel and you don't want all your "personality building" efforts to be devalued by a casual comment left in the wrong place.

You therefore need to protect your on-line identity or reputation. If you want to know more about how you are perceived on-line, it is important to Google yourself often to find out what you're really saying about yourself and what others are saying too. Are you building your brand's reputation in a convincing way? If you were a customer, would you be impressed with the results of your search?

Think about who might Google you, and then create the right messages to attract them. You could also set up an RSS feed or Google Alert for yourself or your business name so you're aware of any new coverage of you as it appears.

Know your Values. What are you really passionate about? What makes you happy? What makes you mad? What fulfils you? In short, what are your values? Take some time to think about the things that really matter to you. It is a great starting point for identifying your ideal way of doing business.

Make a list of all the things really important to you in your life.

For example: to be straightforward, honest, ethical, clear, transparent, friendly, professional, creative, responsible, respectful and flexible.

Which ones are the most important to you in how you conduct your life and your business?

List your Top 5 values here:

1..

2..

3..

4..

5..

It is important that you communicate your values well, not just in your communications but throughout your business. For example, if one of your values is to be an ethical business then this has to shine through in every part of your activity.

 Pret à Manger 'values' fresh food, minimising waste and treating people well. Therefore, all their food is made on the premises and anything left over at the end of the day is given to charities and homeless shelters.

 How do you treat your customers; your staff, your suppliers? The materials used in your store design; products and marketing materials all say something about you, as do the blogs you comment on.

Do you have activities which involve specific ethical practices? If so, publicise them as much as possible in everything you do. Blogs and sites about ethical issues provide a great opportunity to communicate your message further afield than your own website.

The places where your business can communicate these values are called "touchpoints" and we'll look at these in more detail in Section 4, (page 76).

How do you like to work?

Remember the Your Future Life exercise on page 25 where you looked at the future environment you would like to create for yourself. Think now about how you would work within that environment.

Are you a people person? Do you work best alone? Are you always coming up with new ideas? Do you prefer to brainstorm with others? Do you like to analyse a problem? Or do you sleep on it?

 Stelios Haji-Ioannou founder of Easyjet likes to do things in a straightforward and 'easy' way, this eventually became the Easyjet brand, and now we have Easy Cars, Easy Hotels, Easy Pizza etc.

A great way to understand the culture of your business is to spotlight your skills, as this may add another dimension to how you run your business. If you are a people person and can motivate others to come up with solutions to problems, chances are you will create a people-centric culture. If you love to think laterally and you're really good at having ideas, it may be that you create an innovating culture for your brand.

 Spotlight your skills. The real secret to finding your true business strengths is to focus on the skills you like to use and things that you're really interested in.

Don't just focus on what you've done in the past and whether you've enjoyed it or not. If you always do what you've always done, you'll continue to get what you've always had, and this applies to your business as much as to anything else.

Concentrate on what you like to do, not just on what your CV says you can do. Try to be specific. To say that you are a "good communicator" doesn't really throw a lot of light on the subject. However, if you know that you enjoy talking informally to small groups of people but hate making formal presentations, then you're starting to get somewhere.

What are your top 5 skills?

1..

2..

3..

4..

5..

Knowing the environmental qualities that enhance your capabilities is important. Using this knowledge will help create a sense of place, and you will be at ease in that place. You could call this the culture you like to inhabit, and it often brings something important to the essence of your brand.

List your top 5 cultural requirements here

1...

2...

3...

4...

5...

 Your culture plays an enormous part in building your business, so if you say your culture is fast, cutting edge and efficient make sure your office portrays this when you have visitors.
If they're left waiting in the reception area for 15 minutes without an update or refreshments, you've failed already! Likewise how you answer the phone, and how quickly emails are responded to all form part of this picture in the mind of your clients.

Putting it all together with PVC

Before we move on, take a moment to gather your answers to the previous exercises here:

	Personality (page 31)	Values (page 33)	Culture (page 37)
1			
2			
3			
4			
5			

Your PVC (Personality, values and culture) are the key components of your future brand. Using these effectively and communicating them consistently will give you "the difference that makes the difference". You will find out more about how to use your PVC later on in this book.

The Animal Within

'It's a Jungle Out There' is an expression often used to depict the complexity of the market for your products and services: the increasing competition, the pricing strategies required, the right places to sell your goods and ultimate positioning strategy.

It may indeed seem like a jungle for those businesses which do not have a cohesive brand strategy based on their own uniqueness, but for those who have decided to use this to give them competitive advantage, it could seem like a slow, quiet river. Why? Because these people understand 'the difference that makes the difference' when it comes to marketing their products and services.

 This exercise is best done in a quiet place where you can really concentrate. It should be undertaken without too much thought. Usually the first animal you think of is the right one. Work through the questions writing down, or drawing, what comes into your head instinctively. It's very important to be clear but also rich in detail when describing your animal.

- If you could choose one animal to define you in your business environment, what would it be?
- What does it look like?
- What are its behaviour patterns? (Describe fully)
- What is its environment like? (Describe fully)
- How good is it at finding food?
- How does it communicate?

Use the next page to draw or write about your animal and its environment.

Now turn to Appendix 1 on page 131 for some guidance on interpreting your responses. Are there any points here that can clarify your PVC points from the previous exercise?

Summary

In this section you have explored:

- your vision for your future life
- the essential qualities, values and skills that make you who you are
- how those qualities create the unique culture of your business
- your PVC
- your animal within.

Now that you understand these qualities in yourself and your business idea, we can translate them into useful information on how you business works – your brand.

Section 3: Developing your brand with PVC ●●●

You and your
core business idea

Understanding
yourself

Understanding
your business

Developing your
brand with PVC

Building your
brand-led business

Growing your
brand-led business

Action plan and
brand MOT

Understanding the essence of your brand

All human beings are unique. This uniqueness permeates everything we do, from the way we dress to our personal attitudes and beliefs. For a business to become a brand, it has to provide evidence of how it is unique in comparison with its competitors.

The previous section was about YOU and how you want to run your business. This section will show you how the qualities of your personality, values and culture (PVC) translate into tangible aspects of your business and therefore define your brand.

Inward Quality	Outward Expression
Personality	The visual, oral, written and sensory elements of your brand
Values	The unique way that you deliver your particular brand
Culture	Your working environment and company ethos

We run a workshop on this subject called No More Hiding. Why *No More Hiding?* Because gone are the days of concealing your unique qualities, now everyone is going to know about them! When we deliver this workshop to a large group of people, we usually play an old favourite track of ours from Bananarama:

> *"It ain't what you do it's the way that you do it.*
>
> *It ain't what you do it's the time that you do it.*
>
> *It ain't what you do it's the place that you do it,*
>
> *and that's what gets results!"*

The lyrics are very pertinent in today's crowded marketplace. You may have the same product or service as someone just down the road, but if you can present it in a slightly different way, you will draw attention to yourself and, as the song goes: that's what gets results!

The key to PVC is that it is YOU that makes your brand unique. That's what gives power to a brand-led business over a sales-led business. Two companies can make the same product but they can never be the same brand. Someone can attempt to replicate an existing business, but they will never BE that brand.

We like to use an iceberg model to demonstrate how you form a link between who you are and what you are about and how you run your business.

The Cool Tool™

Branding isn't just the outward expression at the tip of the iceberg. Look at the diagram overleaf: under the water level sits your PVC: Personality, Values and Culture. The information you have learnt about yourself so far in this Branding Workshop process is really deep and important stuff, it's the information that makes you different, and forms the foundation of your brand.

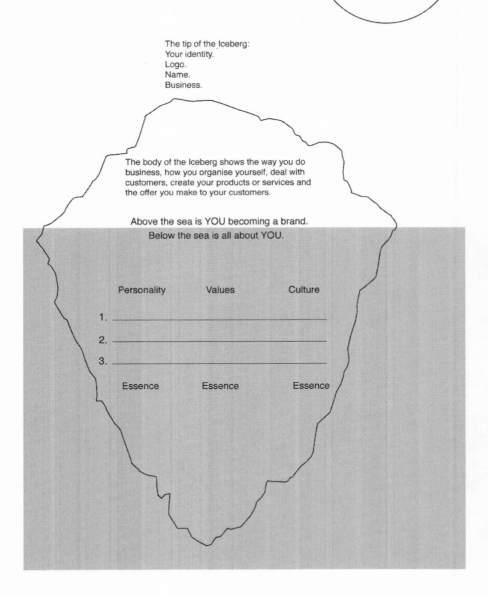

The sun focuses on your communication strategy. The look and feel of your business, eg your packaging and marketing materials and the way you speak to your audience(s), via PR, the web, blogs etc.

The tip of the Iceberg:
Your identity.
Logo.
Name.
Business.

The body of the Iceberg shows the way you do business, how you organise yourself, deal with customers, create your products or services and the offer you make to your customers.

Above the sea is YOU becoming a brand.
Below the sea is all about YOU.

Personality	Values	Culture
1.		
2.		
3.		
Essence	Essence	Essence

In this section you will work on the 5 words you selected for each of the PVC headings in Section 2 and refine them to create statements about your brand which will eventually form the basis of your marketing plan.

 Look back now at your answers in Section 2, you summarized them on page 38.

You have 5 words under each of the headings: personality, values and culture. Think now about which 3 in each category really are the key drivers for you. These words sum up the underpinning knowledge of your brand because they give a sense of who you are and how you operate in your business.

If you need a wider perspective, ask a few people you trust to give you some feedback - which words would they choose? Don't be deflected from what you know to be true about yourself, but use their opinions to gain added insight.

Once you are clear on the 3 words that really matter in each category, fill them in on the iceberg. The 9 words you end up with will be essential for you to focus on as your business grows. They give the bigger picture of YOU and all the things that are particular about you.

Distillation

During the course of this book, you have learnt a lot about yourself and the way you want to work in business. This stage provides you with a funneling process, in order to become really clear in your marketing and communications and in order to think through the way you organise your business. Simplicity is always best.

To do this, you now need to consider the words under each section and choose just 1 under each heading which **really** inspire you to move forward. These are uniquely YOU and will become your future brand essence.

In the fast-moving world that we now live in, customers like bite-sized chunks of information. Perhaps 3 simple words that sum up a brand. You may find it useful to push yourself in the shoes of you customers and see if you can distill your PVC into 3 key words that describe your brand.

This stage provides you with the essence of your brand. It's like taking half a field of lavender to make a bottle of essential oil. The three words you choose should have potency. Don't rush, these words are important. Sometimes it's good to sleep on it, as time can bring more clarity to your thinking.

These are uniquely YOU and will become your future brand essence.

Taking your essence into your brand

Remember that Bananarama song? It ain't just what you do, it's the way that you do it...well these 3 essence words are the way that YOU do it! They are the essence of your brand-led business, and are the means by which you can take the qualities of what is essentially YOU into your brand, and make your business unique.

For example, if 'dynamic' is the essence of your personality, think about how you demonstrate that through all areas of your business. How does being dynamic show itself in the way you structure your business, the way you deal with customers, your products or service, and your sense of identity?

This next stage takes your 3 essence words and starts to tease them out into demonstrable activities that will be tangible to clients. They form the building blocks of your brand, and can be used to create a manual of the way you want to do things.

Taking your essence into your business. This exercise will start to expand your 3 essence words into statements of intent ie how you will deliver your brand through your business.

For each of your essence words, think about how you will demonstrate this throughout your business, in your organizational structure, marketing, products and services, customer relations and sense of identity.

For example

Personality	**Dynamic**	create a buzz marketing campaign locally
		business organised so I can take on new ideas quickly and communicate them with gusto to our customers
		our brand will develop speaking opportunities at the key events this year in our market sector to establish our name in the marketplace quickly
Values	**Sustainable**	we will form sustainable relationships with our local suppliers based on "fair-trading" principles in order to jointly develop innovative products and services to our customers
Culture	**Creative**	all our staff will work in one large room to create an open dialogue on new product development
		once a month, we will hold a one-day brainstorming session with all staff and key suppliers to discuss new ideas

Now it's your turn:

Personality		
Values		
Culture		

These three essential words can be used to form brand differentiation, or a brand statement that is easy to remember. It becomes a touchstone for you and your team to remind you of the essential qualities of your brand. This statement is really for your internal use, you may develop it later into a slogan or tag line intended for external communication.

The Branding Workshop studies models of branding used by the big agencies, and creates simple models to make branding accessible to any size of client, not just corporates.

Personality	**Simple**	we take complex ideas and language and turn them into simple statements and methods
Values	**Effective**	we choose the most useful tools and leave out others over the years we have learnt what really works for our customers
Culture	**Fun**	we use workshops, creative engagement, laughter

At The Branding Workshop, our brand differentiation statement is 'simple, effective and fun'.

What happens if you already have a Brand?

It's really important to re-evaluate your brand from time-to-time and to revisit your PVC, and you can use the process in this section to audit what currently exists. You could even ask some of your employees, suppliers and customers to take part. You can ask them how they perceive you, both positively and negatively, and see what that tells you.

As brands are very much held in the mind of the customer, it is good to evaluate these areas. You could compare what they tell you with your own perceptions and then conduct a 'gap analysis' - is there a gap between what their perceptions are and what yours are. If so, you need to bring them into line, see where they fit and where the gaps are. You can then decide the actions you must take to rectify things.

The Brand MOT in Section 6 (page 112) will also be especially relevant to you.

Brand Positioning

Now that you understand YOU and how the essence of your PVC affects every aspect of your business, you can start to work on building your brand. The next step is to think about the way in which your brand is (or will be) seen. This is called brand positioning.

Brand positioning is the way in which your customers perceive your brand in relation to others and establish an opinion about it. You can see, therefore, that it is like forming a relationship with someone. You meet them and immediately begin to weigh up your thoughts about them. A brand has to decide the type of opinion it would like its customers to have and create strategies through its PVC to do so.

As customers interact with your brand, they begin to compare you to other brands they know or use. As they compare your brand to another one, they begin to form a mental hierarchy of the attributes they like about your brand and those they want to buy into, for example, why do some people prefer to shop in Waitrose rather than Sainsbury's? It is very important for you to understand your customers and what makes them tick.

In a crowded marketplace a small business is able to work very closely with its customers to deliver their requirements and by so doing offer very strong positioning statements.

For some customers a local producer is more desirable than a national one, so if one of your "culture" qualities is 'customer-focused', it will be a great positioning statement to say, "we deliver locally". If you state that you "take care of the local environment", make sure that you are visible at local environmental events such as sponsoring a river cleaning day, or a local fund-raising event to raise money for an ecological project.

International brands have to use more global positioning statements to satisfy wider audiences. They can make grand claims such as "Never Knowingly Undersold" because they can deliver. Small businesses must be careful to position themselves correctly.

 Brand Positioning: bringing the brand statement to life. Brand positioning is about the opinion you want your customers to form about your brand, the following questions will help you to formalise your future positioning for your brand-led business. If you have an existing business, use this process as a review, for a new business, this is about envisioning the future.

What would you like your customers to miss the most if your brand wasn't around?

What would be your brand's most important benefits to its customers?

What value will your brand deliver to its customers? (remember your value qualities in the PVC)

What stories do you want to create about your brand?

How will your brand inspire others?

What do your competitors do that you would never do?

What would you do that your competitors would never do?

 You can now develop your answers into a statement that solidifies what you now know about your brand. This "brand positioning statement" will summarise the key benefits of your brand to your specific audience.

What is your offer?	
What are its key benefits?	
Who are you talking to?	

Here is a brand positioning statement from The Branding Workshop:

 We offer branding solutions for everyone.

Its benefits are that it's simple, effective and fun.

We are talking to small businesses from individuals, micros to medium-sized businesses.

The Brand Promise

When a business engages with its customers there is a form of contract between them. A brand-led business is very consistent in how it works with this relationship ie it makes a promise to its customers.

Having created a brand positioning statement you can enhance this into what we call a 'Brand Promise'. The Brand Promise is a statement from you to your customers that tells them what they should expect from all interactions with your brand. This is the heart of your business. It can be implicit, embedded in everything you do.

In the Branding Workshop, we try to make branding 'simple, effective and fun' and attainable to all, for small businesses. That is both our Brand Statement and our Brand Promise, but for larger organizations, the statement may only be internally referenced and the promise externally stated.

 Use your Brand Promise and positioning statement to develop a tag line. Now think about a phrase that gets to the heart of what you want your customers to feel, experience and expect from your brand. Remember that your brand exists in the minds of your customers, and if you don't create a tag line, they might! Better to be in control.

 John Lewis promise that their goods are 'never knowingly undersold'. This sums up price points and customer service in one clear statement. Remember that John Lewis's organisational structure is managed in such a way that it can fulfil its brand promise. Make sure yours is achievable given the nature of your business.

So now it's over to you...

Make your promise catchy and memorable, and see if you can shorten it to 2 or 3 words.

Developing Emotional Closeness with your customers

Now that you have created a Brand Positioning Statement and a Brand Promise, you need to get close to those valuable customers. This next part of your positioning focuses on emotional closeness. This is the key to a brand's success. It is a way of showing your customers that you really value them, you really understand them, and you are there for them. You now need to work out how you will build the qualities below into your strategy. There are 5 elements in this which will help you breathe life into the brand.

Intimacy/Rapport

What methods can you use to develop a personal intimacy or rapport with your customers, so that they feel you really understand them? Can your brand deliver intimate moments with your clients? Inviting them for breakfast, lunch or coffee is great way to do this.

You can find out more about your customers, their birthdays, their families, their interests. Think about what you talk to your hairdresser about? Perhaps they have your date of birth and send you a treatment voucher for your birthday.

Moo makes it very easy for you to order your personalised items on-line, which allows them to process bigger volumes at lower cost than if each customer spoke to a member of staff. Ordering products through some similar sites feels impersonal. But Moo takes every opportunity to build rapport and soften the process. When you place an order with them you receive this message:

"I'm Little MOO - the bit of software that will be managing your order with us. I will shortly be sent to Big MOO, our print machine who will print it for you in the next few days. I'll let you know when it's done and on its way to you."

Loyalty

Genuine customer loyalty is about a lot more than points on a Nectar card. Perhaps a free coffee at your local deli isn't worth as much as your Air Miles account, but if it's served with style and personality, then the occasional treat feels like a genuine reward for your custom.

How can you really give your customers something to let them know you appreciate their loyalty? Something that will in turn build further loyalty from them?

 In France, the local supermarket has a 'Junior Club'. Each time a child has a birthday, they receive a voucher the week before with a great call to action, "ring our Patisserie Chef NOW to discuss which FREE birthday cake you would like to share with your family!"

Reputation

Some companies seem to gain a reputation very quickly. Why do you think that is? Sometimes it's due to good service, sometimes its due to a trend that's really taken off, sometimes it's just that "je ne sais quoi" – that's great branding! Brand reputation is difficult to attain, but once you've got it, hold onto it, don't cut back on those little details that got you that reputation in the first place! The better the reputation you have, the more customers will tell others about you and the more they will seek you out. This is what's called a 'pull' strategy, which we'll discuss later on page 92.

 Anita Roddick built the reputation of The Body Shop by never testing on animals, which was a fresh innovation at the time. The Body Shop has always stayed true to that ethos.

Empathy

You might think that a positioning based on empathy is difficult to attain, but it is not. Which brands do you know who have a unique empathy with their customers? A specific service industry that accentuates empathy is the 'well-being' sector. Not only in terms of the services it offers, but the way it treats its customers. It may be as simple as offering a gown for use when having to change for a treatment, playing relaxing music at the dentist or offering a sensory experience in the waiting room to relax and unwind the customer.

 Neal's Yard always has a herbalist on hand in their shops to assist clients to make the correct choice of product for any ailment they may have.

Commitment

An effective branding strategy begins with a strong organisational commitment to using your unique brand PVC effectively and consistently throughout everything you do.

It is therefore important to tell your staff, suppliers and stakeholders about your key values and explain to them how they should be integrated into their daily routines, their communications with the customer and in the way you work as a team.

 Although everyone moans about their local car repairer, Sue has a great one. He is committed to getting her back on the road as soon as possible. He offers coffee on arrival; then he sits down and explains the problems with the car in everyday language. He has a passion for what he does and when he has finished the work a lovely new air freshener is hanging in my car as a gift. That's what we call commitment.

Respect

Which brands do you truly respect? It's like any relationship; trust is a large part of respect. Respect is the ultimate accolade a brand can have. Every interaction with your customer is an opportunity to create a lasting positive, respectful relationship that will serve you well in your development towards your brand goals.

Yes, respect is a two-way relationship with the brand. If you respect your customers, your customers will respect you! Many brands fall flat when they start using messages that patronise their customers. Remember people aren't stupid; they can spot a lie a mile-off!

 Divine Chocolate set out to bring fairness to the cocoa producers of its chocolate whom now own 45% of the whole business.

Big brands spend a lot of money striving to achieve these attributes, but small brands stay closer to their customers and can offer these qualities in the natural course of their business.

These mechanisms will give you opportunities to deliver your brand promise is a way that is genuinely memorable to your customers and is likely to generate word of mouth referrals.

Which brands form emotional connections for you? List some brands you admire in the first column, then think about the emotional keywords you associate with the brand, and the results.

Brand	Emotional keyword	Result
eg Co-Operative Supermarket	Commitment	Committed to local suppliers
	Respect	Treats suppliers well

5 C's: Your daily branding workout

Having worked with many businesses, we've identified 5 qualities which are crucial to success for any brand. If you take these on board, your brand will shine.

Credibility: How can you persuade the market to do business with you, instead of your competition? Does your company deliver what it says it will deliver?

Credibility is the ultimate shortcut in the consumer's decision-making process. If you are a producer of vegan cakes, does the Vegan Society recognise you?

Congruence: Do you walk your talk? Is your brand in alignment with your beliefs and values and does everybody that works for you understand them? Believe them? Communicate them in the way they deliver your service? Big companies call this their brand culture.

If one of your core beliefs is that of "family values" but you don't offer your own staff paternity leave, then you're not being congruent. If you believe in having business integrity, you will pay your suppliers in full on time. That is being congruent.

Consistency: At its highest level this means ensuring consistency of the customer's experience with the brand. Are all your visual communications consistent in their style?

If you produce chocolates do they always taste exactly the same? If you offer a service, is the experience of your service the same for all your customers?

Coherence: Means that your customers understand what you are trying to say. Your messages need to be clear, targeted and in a language that your customers will understand.

Tesco use the message "Every Little Helps" and demonstrate that through all the offers they make to their customers.

Connection: Is about how brands make their customers feel. Every time a brand speaks, it signals what we can expect to feel when we experience the brand. Starbucks is a good example of this. They have created their cafés to feel like a "home from home" wherever you are in the world.

 Take a look back at the brands you listed in the previous exercise, can you identify these 5 qualities in them?

Brandstories

These are a series of short stories which give your brand relevance to a particular target market or audience. The stories can be about the company, its products and innovations or its people. Brandstories are built on the foundation of connecting people through a story that is relevant, real and repeatable. Repeatability is the key.

Your story needs to be clear and understandable otherwise it will not have that 'repeatability'. You may have often heard people say, "Oh, we don't do any marketing." and you invariably know what they are going to say next? "Our marketing is all word of mouth."

Well, brandstories ARE word of mouth but in a different way, brandstories are a form of viral marketing. They rely on people talking about you, repeating your story, and they also rely on the people saying that you are someone to be trusted.

When Jamie Oliver recommends a particular farm to buy your sausages from, the sausages fly off the shelves because Jamie is a great brandstory teller.

With Harley Davidson's brand stories the lawyer escapes his high-stress job to experience the freedom of the open road This relates back to Harley's key values: fierce individuality; rebellion against things that are unjust; free spirited and wild.

Good brandstories are comprised of a number of elements that combine to form a strong story. These stories can take a number of forms, including press releases, presentations, case studies, podcasts and videos.

The key to a good brandstory – just like good cooking – is to break down your story to simple ingredients and make sure that they are assembled the same way every time.

Eight Steps to Brandstory Success:

1. Make it Desirable.

2. Make it Clear.

3. Make it Relevant.

4. Make it Real.

5. Make it Memorable.

6. Make it Repeatable.

7. Make it Rewarding.

8. Last by no means least, make it Repeatable.

As you can see repeatability is the key!

 Innocent, a UK drinks company making 100% natural and organic smoothies, launched the Big Knit campaign in 2003. Every winter their drinks in selected locations sport tiny hand-knitted hats, and for every bottle sold with a hat they make a donation to Age Concern and Age UK who help keep older people warm and healthy through the winter months.

In 2011, the overall campaign is set to the £1million mark with 650,000 hats knitted by individuals and groups up and down the country. Over 80% of the hats are produced in groups within Age UK centres by people who benefit directly from the funds raised.

Not only does this campaign capture the public's imagination, but it also associates Innocent with good cause marketing.

Brandstories don't have to be elaborate. Original ideas come from clever thinking, not big research budgets. Clients often say to us, "but we're not Nike, how can we build a brand without their budget?" The answer is: get creative! The price of original thinking could be a few drinks with friends, coming up with ideas. And, yes, the implementation of some of these ideas will need a budget, but not always!

Whether you intend it or not, a story already exists in the mind of your customers

 Find out more about your current reputation from those who count the most, your target audience. Set up a simple questionnaire to ask your customers about your product or service - don't just assume you know what they think!

If you have a retail business, an interesting printed card could be a good idea, or look at online options such as Survey Monkey and MailChimp.

Alternatively you can test your existing market by sampling it with new products. This is particularly successful if you can give them testers of food, beauty products, etc.

Perhaps it would also be fun to be a mystery shopper for a day and go and see how your products (or your competitors') are being sold in other stores?

Once you have carried out some research on your products or services you can then start to improve how they are marketed. If you are running a small company, you probably won't have a huge marketing budget, so why don't you start telling stories, and we don't mean porky pies. We mean Brandstories.

If there is a significant gap between the answers from your customers and your vision for your business, this points to where you need to work to communicate your ideas more effectively.

Develop your own Brandstory This will become a story you can tell about your business, one of your products/services, or the way you work with a particular supplier.

Consider Innocent's above. How can you capture your customers' imagination with an interesting story which could develop into some sort of promotional exercise? What sort of story would be interesting for your customers? How could you bring it to life and make it memorable in the minds of your customers? Think 'outside the box'.

Here are some pointers to get you started:

Have you recently had to personalise an order for your products or services? How did you deal with that?

Have you recently done something "local" to help the community?

Do your products have interesting raw ingredients which could be interesting to talk about?

Remember that a good story has human interest, and includes an unexpected element, a new way of doing things.

 Mongoose is a manufacturer of innovative cricket equipment. Building entirely on fans' interest in their game-changing bat, the brand has quickly grown to include a full range of cricket equipment.

Your Brand Checklist

Well done! Having completed the previous exercises, you now have a full picture of the components that make up your brand.

Your brand checklist now becomes your guide as you go forward to build your brand-led business in the next section.

Go back through the answers to your exercises now and fill in the chart below. Photocopy this page and use it as a reminder about the core of your business, because your brand is the core of how YOU do business.

Personality	1
	2
	3
Values	1
	2
	3
Culture	1
	2
	3
Brand Essence: Personality	
Brand Essence: Values	
Brand Essence: Culture	
Positioning Statement (internal)	Offer:
	Key benefits:
	To whom:
Brand Promise (external)	

Summary

In this section you have:

- explored how the qualities of YOU identified in Section 2 translate into the PVC (personality, values, culture) of your brand
- used PVC to lead you to the essential qualities of your brand
- used this to understand your brand positioning and create your brand promise
- seen how these allow you to develop emotional connections with your clients
- understood the 5 C's of branding
- used that information to create your brand story/stories
- put everything into a summary page you can use in your marketing plans

You are now ready to build your business!

Section 4: Building your brand-led business ●●●

You and your
core business idea

Understanding
yourself

Understanding
your business

Developing your
brand with PVC

Building your
brand-led business

Growing your
brand-led business

Action plan and
brand MOT

Overview

In the previous sections you've covered all the foundation work, and now it's time to integrate the thinking you have done about your brand into your business. Businesses have to be built brick-by-brick and we have developed this simple chart to show you the building blocks you will need.

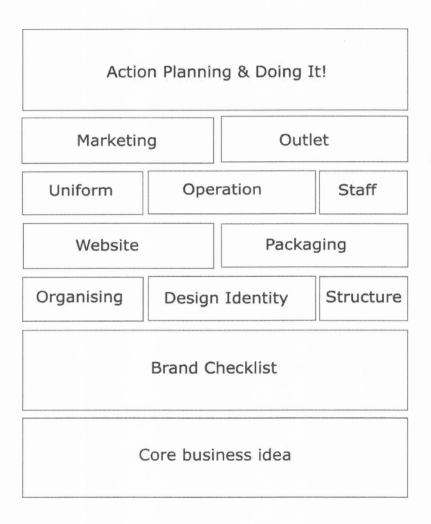

Action Planning & Doing It!

Marketing

Outlet

Uniform

Operation

Staff

Website

Packaging

Organising

Design Identity

Structure

Brand Checklist

Core business idea

Your core business idea now has the Brand Checklist to support it and you are ready to move forward and make all this information work for your business.

Design

On the surface, design is the visual manifestation of your brand's personality. Then as you dig deeper into a design strategy your values and culture become more evident. Using your Brand Checklist as a base, you can now develop a great brief to give to a graphic designer, web-site designer, product designer or interior designer because you can give them something which encapsulates all your thinking about your brand.

 Take a moment to list the places where your brand will be visible. Think about business cards, logo, stationery, website, uniforms, vehicles and more.

You will see that there are lots of places where you can claim the interaction with your client and use it to reinforce your brand values. Whether you intend to use a designer or to create some or all of these aspects yourself, the next stage in the process will focus your ideas and help develop consistency.

Develop your mood

What sort of mood or universe can you imagine for your business? Everything you use from the colours on your business card to your choice of paint will communicate something about you.

You may have already thought of some great images to sum up your vision. If not, try the collage technique from Section 2 to develop some 'mood boards'. If you are a fashion designer, what fabrics might sum up your products? What type of fashion era, epoch, imagery or graphics could be appropriate?

If you chose to create a collage in the Your Future Life exercise in back in Section 2 (page 25), use it now to help develop ideas for the mood of your brand. The look and feel you created then came straight from YOU and will contain valuable insights that you can use here. This can then be applied to the interior of your shop, your packaging or your on-line or printed communications.

If you didn't do a collage in Section 2 start by ripping up magazines, bits of packaging, photographs, scraps of fabric, flyers and postcards. Gather them into ideas on colours, textures, shapes. A professional mood board would present these as neat samples, but the important part is the research. A collection of themed references and images in an old envelope will still give a designer a great place to start, so don't worry if they're not laid out nicely!

If you have a health food shop – are you rustic or are you pure? How do these qualities look to you: brown paper and wood or crisp white and stainless steel? If you are a complementary therapy practitioner, do you want to be seen as professional or caring, or 'alternative'? Your Branding Checklist will help you edit and select ideas that align with your PVC.

These mood boards can be very helpful to help you develop a visual identity for your business. Knowing your 'mood' visually will be very useful in your choice of imagery and typestyle. You now know that branding is so much more than your logo, and that your identity should portray the 'essences' of your brand thinking. The mood boards are the first step.

The next step is to decide on a typeface(s), colours, styles of layout, images, materials etc that communicate your brand through the various mechanisms you listed above. The elements that you need to define will depend on the nature of your business.

You may want to do this with a designer, or you may be doing it on your own, or with friends/ business partner(s). If you're working with a designer, the mood boards and brand checklist form a great basis from which they can start to understand you and your brand. As a small business you may be using the expertise of an assortment of friends and relatives to get you going. Having a clear sense of the qualities which underpin your brand means the various elements can still be visually related even if they're created by a number of different people.

The main thing is that once you have developed a brand identity, you or your designer(s) should develop brand identity standards which will apply to all designed elements. For instance, the colours, typestyles, formats you have chosen in your identity should apply consistently throughout all of your printed and on-line marketing communications. This is what we call visual cohesion. These standards can take the form of a few printed pages of guidelines, through to a large corporate manual. It's important to explain these standards carefully to your suppliers such as printers, producers etc.

The way you (and your staff) talk to clients is also important. Make sure the degree of formality suits the personality of your brand and that all your communications match. An ill-considered blog post can undo months of painstaking work in a click.

Your brand rituals

We spoke about brand rituals in Section 1 (page 19) and now that you've developed your brand definition, you can think about ways in which rituals apply to you.

As well as the obvious items like business cards, signage, packaging and so on, there are many other places where you can bring an emotional connection into play. Think about your product or service at all 'touchpoints' with the consumer. Each of these provides an opportunity for you to create a memorable symbol, ritual, or way of using your product that could make the brand more memorable. It might be as simple as putting something unusual on the saucer of a cup of coffee: a beautiful little hand-made cookie rather than a standard chocolate with some-one else's brand name on the wrapper.

Use the following questions to think this through and generate ideas:

Do you have a particular way of doing things?

Are there any rituals already associated with your product or service?

Is there a manner in which customers must open or use your product?

Is there an interesting way for you to "make your mark" with your customer?

Is there an opportunity for you to develop a memorable symbol or sound associated with your product or service?

Organising your Business

As well as your brand identity your brand thinking also informs the way you run your business. Using this, you can create a potent vision that sums up the Core Business Idea you have for your business.

Larger companies sometimes have a framed Vision (or Mission) Statement in their reception areas so everyone who enters the building or works there remembers what the company stands for. Even for a smaller business, it's not a bad idea for you to communicate your vision somewhere in your working environment to remind you and your staff of what you're aiming to deliver. For The Branding Workshop our vision is to 'empower small businesses' by making branding accessible to them. We do this by making branding simple, effective and fun (see page 54).

The Vision is the starting point for what you want your business to achieve. Ideas you put into developing your brand positioning and brand promise can now be delivered through your vision.

 What is your Vision? Develop a sentence that describes your vision for your business. Make sure it is distinctive, something you passionately believe in and that is desirable to your customers. It may help you to look back at the first exercise (page 25) Your Future Life, as your business vision needs to be in alignment with this thinking.

eg Ikea: good design for all.

Business strategy

Your business consists of many elements; such as how you organise yourself, your business processes, the finance in your business, and your marketing and sales strategy.

Many books have been written on these subjects and we are not going to address them all here, but something that is really important to consider is how you market, based on the techniques used in this book (coming up in Section 5).

Brand-led marketing will grow your business. It doesn't matter whether you are a small business just starting out or one that has been established for a while, you want to make sure that all your activities are aligned through your brand. So first let's look at areas you need to consolidate in order to be confident that growth will sustain its essential qualities.

SWOT

A SWOT is a strategic analysis or overview of the Strengths, Weaknesses, Opportunities and Threats that exist for an organisation or individual. It allows you to look down on the on the internal and external factors effecting your business.

If you are already running a business, or just starting one, this is a very good exercise to do. Having gathered a lot of information about your business over the previous sections, now is a good time to use this marketing tool to analyse your current position.

If you'd like more guidance, take a look on-line, where you will find many examples of how to carry out a SWOT. One website we like which gives you a great introduction is www.mindtools.com.

A SWOT is a great way to highlight your strengths which will include your skills, but also your weaknesses, which may mean that you need to learn new skills or new ways of doing things, thus turning them into opportunities to change the way you work.

Strengths	Weaknesses
What advantages do you have?	*What could you improve?*
What do you do better than others?	*What should you avoid?*
Opportunities	**Threats**
What trends are you aware of?	*What are your competitors doing?*
How are customers changing?	*What changes in legislation might affect your business?*

Use the examples shown to get you started. Be succinct with your answers and make sentences if possible to clarify your thinking.

Then see how each part can have an impact on your business (negative or positive).

- What can you do to make the most of the opportunities and strengths?
- How can you strengthen your weaknesses?
- How can you counteract the threats posed by external factors?

PESTEL

While a SWOT gives you a good overview of your business, a PESTEL analysis looks at the market conditions surrounding your business.

It is good to be conversant with this technique as well, as it is a great way to really do some focused research and find out what factors might change your territory. Having an awareness of these aspects of the market conditions will give you a strong basis from which to respond to changes and developments as your business grows.

Political	
Economic	
Social	
Technological	
Environmental	
Legal	

Organisational Strategy

Look back at your brand checklist (page 68), where you summarised the key elements of your brand. As you grow your business, your staff and associates will have to understand, assimilate and deliver all your brand facets to your customers. As the owner of the business, it is your job to inspire them to do so and at least initially, manage the process.

 Pret a Manger recruit specifically so that customers get an cheery upbeat welcome as they approach the counter. 'Pret Behaviours' are listed under the Jobs section at www.pret.com, a great insight into the thinking behind the brand.

 Your organisational thinking will depend on the size of your business. You may be a sole proprietor in which case YOU are the internal structure, but you may rely on outside help for certain services or production processes. In which case, these elements will apply directly to you.

Vision: Look back at the Vision exercise on page 78. As you grow a business, one of your key tasks will be to inspire those who work with you to buy into your vision.

If your vision is to be an innovating brand, bringing new ideas to a marketplace, you could set up regular brainstorming sessions with your team. Make these fun occasions, maybe away from the usual workplace, where any idea is up for discussion, and no judgment is given. This way you will harness everyone's creative thinking.

Behaviour: Look back at your Brand Checklist (page 68) and especially at the Brand Essence 'Values'. This will be the way you need to behave in your business and must be integrated into your company's culture both internally with your staff and externally with your customers. This is a big part of 'living the brand'.

Values inform behaviour. If one of your values is to always give outstanding service, are your staff empowered to rectify the situation if a customer complains?

Staff and Recruitment: You may need to recruit staff to help you on a full-or part-time basis. If you do, remember the qualities needed to communicate the uniqueness of your brand.

 If you are a website development company and your brand promise is to make the design process as simple as possible for clients to understand, don't employ a (brilliant) designer who can't communicate without using jargon.

Internal Communication: Remember to keep your staff informed of all activities that relate to your brand. These could be planned developments within the company, or external events.

 Keep everyone up to date on the latest industry news, market changes, new competitors. That way they will be able to speak to your customers in an informed manner, abreast of what is happening and aware of new developments.

So if your cultural value was "easy communication style" make sure that your staff understand your communications, that you speak in a clear manner and bring out the important factors. Then they will understand how they can have an effect on your brand values.

Reward and Recognition System: No matter how small your company is, your staff will work better if they are recognised for their efforts. Get your team involved, give them recognition for their work, and you will develop a great brand culture.

Organise a monthly or quarterly lunch or breakfast briefing, where staff feel they have a forum to voice their opinions or suggestions, positive or negative! If you run a medium-sized business there may be other incentives you can offer to bring in new clients or to develop ideas for growth of the business. If your Value was Recognising Hard Work, make sure the rewards you give are relevant and pertinent to your employee's position in the company. This means that you need to know your staff in order to give them an appropriate incentive.

Training and Development: Even if you are in business as a 'one man band' don't forget about training and development. These areas can get neglected when you are busy running a business, but it is very important to keep your skills and knowledge up to date with Continuing Professional Development.

Join the recognised body for your specialism, so you and your staff can benefit from attending seminars or workshops. Investment in your staff's progress is also a great recognition system. Your staff will feel valued, and if the training helps them move on to other positions in your company where they can spotlight their new skills, that's great for brand-building too. If one of your cultural values is "personal development", a weekly staff yoga class could be as beneficial as a management course.

Creation of Products and Services: You might already have a great product, or range of products, but don't neglect new product development. Keep ahead of your competitors, rather than copy them. Visit the latest trade shows for your industry and see what new products are being spotlighted. There are some great 'trend-spotting' web sites, check them out and think about how your product lines could be developed for these new 'blue-sky' areas.

Hold creative workshops with your staff and/or your suppliers and mind-map or brainstorm new ideas. They're great for thinking about new ways of doing things. To follow up, you can dedicate a member of each group to research a particular area in relation to the development of their product or new target audience.

Develop quality standards for your products and services, i.e. no product, delivery or proposal to any client should leave the building until it has been thoroughly checked. That way you keep your company's standards high for both product and service.

Look into European Standards and ISO quality standards too, or the standards that affect your particular industry or specialism, these are important, particularly when pitching for larger public projects.

The brand guidelines developed earlier apply here too. Make sure all new staff are aware of them in terms of your product as well as your communications.

So if your personality value was Creative - how can you keep your brand personality fresh and creative whilst conforming to standards, regulations and your brand guidelines?

Operations/logistics: New suppliers can offer you a new way of looking at production deadlines, storage, delivery and logistics.

 Who is in charge of this area in your company? Make sure they keep up to date on new operational trends etc. If one of your Values is Respect For People, make sure you use your suppliers and staff to help with your innovation by holding joint brainstorming sessions on all of these logistical aspects of your business.

Distribution channels: Today many companies and brands are engaging in 'Partnership Marketing', 'Marketing Alliances', and 'Strategic Partnerships'. The true success of brand partnerships lie in their power to open up new and alternative channels of distribution for both the companies and the brands involved.

 Think about other channels where you could distribute your products or services. Could you join forces with other companies to offer a joint promotion and therefore distribution channel? Make sure though, that the potential partners you talk to reflect your own brand culture and underpin your own brand values.

 Buddha Bar originally developed in Paris as a music venue and label, now has formed a world-wide partnership with Hilton Hotels to offer Buddha Bar Spas with a range of Zen services.

Franchising and Licensing

As you develop your business, and embed your PVC into it, you will develop a way of doing things: "the way we do things round here". So, as we've seen, every time you walk into a Pret a Manger shop, you get this happy, upbeat welcome.

Once you have established a business in whatever you do - a pizza restaurant, a clothing line, or a business like Stagecoach that teaches drama for children – there are 2 main ways in which you can quickly grow your business: franchising and licensing. Franchising is usually applied to a service and licensing to a creative product. A franchise is basically someone else taking your business into their locality and delivering it in the way that your brand does things.

 The experience of attending a Stagecoach workshop in Surrey, where it started, will be very very similar to attending a Stagecoach workshop in Scotland, or indeed in any of the 10 other countries in which they now operate.

One of the key things that makes franchising possible is that the parent brand has a very strong identity and positioning.

Franchising is one way of growing your brand It is an area that needs careful consideration and planning, so if you think this is an option for you, please seek specific advice.

A second way that you can grow a business is through licensing your brand. Licensing differs from franchising in that you have to own some Intellectual Property (IP). This is something that you have created, such as a set of designs for greetings cards, some textile designs or a product patent.

When you license to another business, you grant them permission to use the IP that you own in exchange for a royalty fee. They generally undertake the production and retail of the product.

 Textile designer Celia Birtwell who created many wonderful designs with her husband Ossie Clarke in the 70s, recently licensed a clothing line to Top Shop and gift items to Boots.

One of the pitfalls is that you have to find a licensing partner that reflects the PVC of your brand in the work that they do. Again this is an area in which you must take expert advice.

 And finally: keep an eye on the competition at all times. What can you add with little cost to make your customers feel that they are getting great value for money? How can you differentiate your offer from your competitors, locally, nationally and globally? Yes, you might be small, but you will probably have global competition. The Internet is just a click away!

Summary

This section has shown you how to use the Brand Checklist
from Section 3 to:

- develop mood boards which reflect what your business
  is about
- use these to brief designers of the visual aspects of
  your business
- understand the business structure and culture that will
  reflect your brand values

You are now ready to reach out and grow your brand-led
business, safe in the knowledge that your foundations are
strongly grounded in the values and ideas that are important
to you.

Section 5:
Growing your brand-led business ●●●

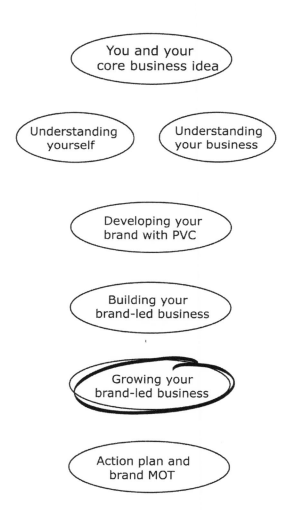

We have now taken you through the branding workshop process to a point where you have a strong understanding of yourself and your brand, and have started to develop ideas of how your brand-led business will operate.

The whole point of doing this work is that it will help you grow your business. Growing your brand-led business relies on marketing your products/services, so this section will look at how you apply your branding knowledge to getting your message across.

How well do you Pull?

Pulling is the key to branding, and it is very different from pushing.

A 'Push' strategy means that you have to go and find your customers. You are constantly using your promotions, marketing strategy and your sales force to create demand for your product. You are in effect 'pushing' your product.

A 'Pull' strategy is one that is built over time by brand reputation. You have consistently developed your brand and created an emotional experience in the minds of your customers so they will come looking for you. Your brand is in effect 'pulling' in your customers.

'Pulling' strategies are based on the credibility and visibility of your product, using visual, sensual, physical experiences.

So how do you pull? It is like being in a bar; are you attractive to who you want to attract? Initially, it may be more of a physical attraction, we see a wonderful product, packaged well – don't you just want to buy it, take it home and then un-wrap it!?

True brand loyalty, however, comes when the relationship between you and the product or service develops – it's just like all human relationships, the more good experiences you have, the more trusting and connected you feel. The aim of the 'pull' strategy in business is to create that connection. The stronger is it, the more repeat business you will have – and that is what we're here for!

Big brands rely on the fact that the more you are loyal to them, the more you will purchase from them. This is why branding is such a commercial business strategy. It's all about creating a deep and lasting 'love or lust' between a brand and its consumer!

What elements of your business would be the most attractive to your customers? At the Branding Workshop we know that our customers value the fact that we simplify branding for them rather than presenting it as a complex subject.

Get a reputation: that's one way to get everyone talking about you!

As we just discussed, credibility and visibility are the cornerstones of developing a reputable brand strategy.

Credibility relates to the product's performance, its style, its reliability, its design, and its purpose. You have to have a credible product before you can give it visibility. In other words, if your product doesn't work, your marketing budget will be completely wasted.

Once you have a credible product, you can give it visibility. This is the experience of using the product, the physical sensations, the product's unique attributes, the way it makes you feel, the way it makes you look.

Bring these two elements of credibility and visibility together and you have reputation, the emotional experience. This is what stays in the mind of your customers time-after-time. This is what brings them back to your hotel. This is what makes them eat your biscuits. This is what makes them take your training course and recommend it to their friends.

Reputation is the ultimate pull strategy!

 Think about your product or service? What do your customers say about it? What do your friends say about it? What does your family say about it? If you don't know, ask!

Want to be Admired?

'Brand admiration' is very important and it's happening all the time. Millions of us are choosing, buying and experiencing brands daily. Whether it's a trip to the cinema, picking up our shopping, or going away for the weekend, we all make decisions based on our emotional experience with the brand.

Brands give us confidence, they become credible in our minds, and they become a brand experience. You may say, well what has a big brand got to do with me. I am a sole trader, a small business with limited budgets. Well all great brands were small brands once. Anita Roddick started The Body Shop from a very small shop in Brighton. Richard Branson started with a small record shop. And Starbucks too...

But, as recently seen in the press, we have a lot to learn from a brand like Starbucks. What makes one of the largest brands on the planet want to un-brand? Change its strategy completely? Emulate the local neighbourhood café with its new concept? It has lost its way, become too big and forgotten its original brand values. This has led to a loss of its unique personality and a lot of market share along the way.

Our Branding workshops have been developed by studying the way big brands operate and what we have done over the last 10 years is to spread our knowledge to everyone in a creative, simple way, and it's worked! There are now some wonderful small brands in existence that we have helped their respective owners to create.

It doesn't matter if you are big or small, you have can have a great brand. You can have a great reputation in just your local area. A reliable plumber, who everyone wants to know about and wants to work with, is a brand in its own right.

Marketing departments are all trying to build great brands that are truly admired above all others. But whilst some brands resonate, many others fail to be noticed, fail to be remembered, and therefore fail to leave a lasting positive emotional impression with us.

 Look back at the brands you listed in the first exercise on page 17. Having worked through this book, do you still admire them? What is it about the way they deliver their brand to you that you admire?

Do you want to be remembered and admired? Take a look at our list below.

Performance: Your profitability or business performance is the most important attribute. If others want to invest in your company, you are developing a winning brand! The emotions this will evoke in your customers will be 'pride' (to be associated with your brand) 'awe' (at your track record) and inclusion (part of the action). They are a part of your success! Richard Branson was the first "personality brand" success story.

Consistency: If your business is consistent in all it does, your communications will be meaningful. This is the key to successful branding and it will bring your staff together with a cohesive vision. This will bring you supreme loyalty and trust. Think of Volvo's adherence to their safety policy.

Credibility: Customers buy your product because the brand means something. They can be sure that they are buying a brand they trust. The more they believe in it and spread the word about you the more credible your brand becomes. This meaning can give your customers a deep sense of place with your brand. The Co-operative bank is a good example of this.

Innovation: Customers can accept change only where the brand values remain the same. So when a brand needs to innovate, it must ensure that it honours its core values. Your customers will have very high expectations and will enjoy using your brand. Apple and Google are good examples.

Inspiration: Make sure you inspire others by keeping one step a head of your competitors. Don't forget to take on board the comments made by your customers too. They can give you great inspirational ideas. Your customers could experience inspiration and creativity with your brand. Maggie's Cancer Care is a great example of this.

These five elements, if considered carefully, will bring admiration to your brand, no matter how big or small it is.

Applying your brand knowledge

In Section 4 you worked on mood boards and design ideas that will inform the look and feel of your brand, now it's time to think about where and how you will apply that knowledge.

If you have a design budget, you'll be handing your mood boards over to an agency, with a list of your needs: business cards, flyers, website etc.

You may not be able to afford outside help at this stage. If you're quite computer-savvy you (or a helpful friend) may be using one or more of the various on-line tools on offer, such as Wordpress, Mailchimp, or the social networks.

These are a great way to develop a low-cost online presence, as long as you apply what you've learnt about your brand and customise their templates to suit your brand identity. Likewise with online printing services for your business cards and stationery: spend a little time making sure all the places where your brand is visible adhere to the brand identity guidelines.

This is not a book on marketing, but here are some key points to consider:

Print: apply all the guidelines you developed in Section 4 to various elements such as: letterheads, invoices, business cards, postcards, flyers, packaging, uniforms, vehicles (possibly including decals for your own car).

 Think about your brand essence and how you can communicate it in print. You might use a unique message or quote on the back of your business cards to make your interactions more memorable. Be sure to give them away generously.

Online: A website is essential, even for a small local business or sole trader. It can just be a few pages, the online equivalent of a basic flyer, or something more elaborate. If possible, use your business name as your web address, and if you're setting up a new business, checking for existing sites with similar names is a good way to help you choose a name.

If you're reasonably comfortable with your computer you can build yourself a site for free. For under £30 a year, you can have a decent site with your own email address such as you@yourbusiness.co.uk, which is much more professional than using a generic email or website service (and be sure to populate the signature with your logo and contact details).

Many small design companies offering great package deals on web site development. Invite some to present their proposals. It might not be as expensive as you think.

If you have a decent budget for on-line marketing, choose a good web-site developer who really knows what they are doing. Look on-line: which web-sites do you admire? Check out who designed and developed them. Who has recently won awards? Do you have friends in business who might recommend someone?

Look for a company which understands the marketing of websites as well as the programming. Having the structure built in the right way will save you money in the long run.

Social Media Marketing

A well-designed website is only effective if it can be found via search engines and social networks. Whether you build your own site or have a professional do it for you, make sure it is listed with Google and other search engines (SEO). You can also use social networks to increase visibility by creating a Facebook page, using Twitter or writing a blog.

Social Media Marketing (SMM) starkly reveals the limits of old (one-way) media, and the power of the Internet (two-way) as a way to reach out to communities.

Initially, marketing on the internet was primarily one-way communication, just like the traditional media of TV, radio, and print. It was simply a new way for a small minority to broadcast a message to a larger group of people. But the internet has always been different from those older communication channels in one critical way: it is capable of accepting input from users and that has opened the doors for the trend of socialization. Socialization on the web is huge already and it's only going to get bigger.

Here are our 10 commandments for using SMM effectively.

- Content builds communities.
- Conversations not shouting.
- Close to your heart communities – because we know each other.
- "What do you want?" *not* "Here's what I've got".
- It's not 'Me *to* You', it's 'Me *with* You'.
- It's informal not formal.
- You can play in other people's spaces and it's OK!
- New World Order – positive communication.
- Your mission (PVC Essences) drives your marketing.
- Surround yourself with content then people can find you!

Look back at your thinking on emotional connections and consider how you can build these into the structure of your on-line presence. Ensure that your Facebook page adheres to the qualities you have identified for your brand, likewise your Tweets and blog posts.

Using interaction, your website becomes much more than a static on-line brochure. Use short on-line surveys to gather customer feedback, send a newsletter, create a members' forum, post information sheets, or video clips. Think of ways your website can be useful and interesting to your clients and your potential clients.

Viral Marketing describes any strategy that encourages individuals to pass on a marketing message to others (remember those brandstories?) This could be a video clip, a voucher, an experience. But remember your PVC at all times and take care to ensure that your various online outlets are in tune with your brand.

Getting your brand out there: Public Relations is simply a means of telling journalists about your business in way that you control. This could be done via a formal press release sent to carefully selected editors. Or it could be a stunt or event specifically designed to attract coverage.

 A woman is walking down the street in a boned, laced bodice. She hands out leaflets to her entranced audience. She makes more than £3,000 in bodice orders within one week. Not bad for an outlay of £70.00 and a couple of hours work.

 We saw a great promotion recently for butter, with two hunky men dressed as cows standing still for hours on fake grass in the metro at Paris. They certainly made an impact!

So, think of interesting ways to get your product out in the street to create a BUZZ!

Something more low-key might suit your brand. Use local organisations as a base for organising a low-cost event. Perhaps they can rent you an unusual venue at a low-cost for a launch with a difference.

Research

Carry out market research regularly on your competitors but also on your industry. Find out the best websites on the issues that concern you and set up RSS feeds on your subjects of interest (see Resources). That way, useful information comes to you daily or weekly and you don't need to go searching for it.

Subscribe to the best industry trade magazines and attend annual trade shows. Visit shops selling your type of products regularly. What's new? What are the trends that you can pick up on and take advantage of? You'll have to be quick if you do it this last way. As we all know trends change FAST.

Remember also that your competitors aren't always competitors, they can also be collaborators, so also note down those you could develop a mutual relationship with.

Use the PESTEL analysis to really find out what your territory is and how far it extends. Who are the competitors you need to watch and learn from, and who are the ones who can learn from you?

YOU

Now that you understand the environment surrounding your business, you still have to come back to you and your role at the heart of your brand. Your expertise is valuable, so get out there and share it. There are lots of ways you could do this: networking; joining associations; commenting on blogs; speaking at meetings and events on radio, in newspapers. Make yourself visible as an expert in your field.

Join professional and social groups on-line and off-line to develop networks and be seen as a professional in your trade or business sector. Volunteer to speak at local group meetings and seminars. Talk with local colleges to offer workshops in your area of expertise. Participate in local community events to enlarge your networking circle and gain brand presence.

Write short articles on your area of expertise and send or email them to relevant trade publications or regional newspapers who like to receive and publish local information.

Promote yourself as an expert and let local media groups know you're available for interviews. Listen to radio talk shows, and when the topic is within your realm of expertise, call in and offer your opinion.

Developing your contacts

So here you are with your brand-led business all set up and ready to roll – who do you tell? You'd be surprised how many people you already know, and how many of them are potential clients, not to mention the people that they know - so let's get marketing!

Throughout our lives, we build up a database of people we know. We keep fragments of this data in different address books, notebooks, our heads, our on-line databases and social media accounts, an interesting card stuck on our notice board.

We don't very often sit down and collate all the contacts we have, but a Contact Tree is like a mind map of all the people you know. Take a look at the following tree and add your contacts to it.

Firstly, write down all the people who first pop into your head: friends, business contacts, colleagues at work, people you meet in the evening socially, people you meet everyday in your local shop, anyone who could be interesting because of who they are, or who they may know, or the databases they may keep etc.

Keep filling in the tree following the branches, smaller branches and smaller still. Here is a captive audience for your product, an audience easy to tap, because they know you, or know of you, or will easily know you (via your contacts). Did you realise how many people you know?

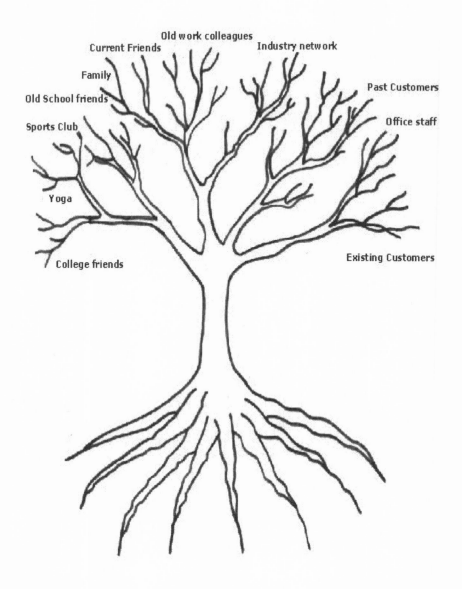

Old work colleagues
Current Friends
Industry network
Family
Past Customers
Old School friends
Office staff
Sports Club
Yoga
College friends
Existing Customers

Now you know who they all are, make sure you keep in contact with them regularly. Over time, you will build a stronger relationship with them. Remember what we said about developing a newsletter? This is a perfect way of developing a relationship marketing communication (just remember to give them the option to unsubscribe – see Permission Marketing in Resources).

Summary

In this section we have looked at ways of growing your brand-led business ie marketing.

- Seen that pulling depends on reputation ie credibility combined with visibility
- Looked at ways to apply brand knowledge: print, online, PR, research, YOU
- Developed your contact tree

You are now ready to take this information forward into the reality of your day-to-day working life.

Section 6:
Action plan and brand MOT ●●●

You and your
core business idea

Understanding
yourself

Understanding
your business

Developing your
brand with PVC

Building your
brand-led business

Growing your
brand-led business

Action plan and
brand MOT

Action Plan and Doing It!

If you are new to business, we suggest you develop an Action Plan that will encapsulate and work towards the elements you thought about in the Vision exercise earlier (page 78).

It will also help you to start marketing your business using your Brand Thinking strategy taken from your Branding Checklist. This will allow you to test the water and see how credible your offer is to your customers. The action plan could include developing a web site, producing a customer service charter, packaging your products etc.

An action plan is simply:

- What am I going to do?
- By when am I going to have done it?

SMART targets are:

- Specific
- Measurable
- Achievable
- Realistic
- Time-bound

and presented in a simple one-liner.

Your most important daily action-goal: Smile, with a deep breath, and affirm your goals.

Make sure your SMART action plan covers all the relevant activities we've talked about so far. You might then want to pull them all together on planner - either online or on paper.

Create your SMART Action Plan

Action	SMART target
Develop website	S: I need on-line trading M: My budget is £500 A: I can use template software R: I have a friend who can help me T: It has to be done by the end of April

Practice achievement and boost your confidence! A good way to start is to set a short term goal to achieve in your business. If you find setting goals difficult, maybe you could talk to a friend about how they set up in business or read some of the wonderful business biographies on such brands as Virgin, Richer Sounds etc.

Once you have reached that first goal, take a moment to consider what you did, how you did it and how it will enhance the overall organizational plans. You will see immediately that your efforts have made a difference.

Then, set a new and slightly more challenging goal, when you reach or exceed this one, you will find that your accomplishments grow and multiply, and you will become more confident in dealing with larger challenges.

The first thing you will notice as you feel more confident is how other people treat you. People will smile at you as you show your inner glow through your own smile. You will be given more respect and your ideas will receive the attention they deserve. Your enjoyment of work and of life will increase many times over. Life will definitely become more interesting, and more fun.

Practice achievement and boost your self confidence today. Wear a smile, and hold your head high. Look other people in the eye when you speak to them, and they will respect you for what you have to say. Self confidence can be developed, and can take your life and business to much greater heights.

Moving Forward

Once your brand is established and well communicated within its target market and sales are going well, you will know that your brand strategy has worked.

You will sometimes embark on a trip of self-doubt, what if the market turns, what if your consumers lose faith in your brand, the product, and perhaps more to the point, what is the competition devising in response to you taking their market share?

It's also easy to become complacent. Your company is doing just fine thanks. But don't rest on your laurels. You have to realise that branding is an ongoing project and passion. There is a need to stay proactive, to keep ahead of the market and your competitors, this is where conducting a Brand MOT once a year is vital.

Brand Review/ MOT

It's important to review your Action Plan and the results of your marketing efforts after 3 months and see if there are any adjustments that need to be made to the Branding Checklist. You can also then amend your Action Plan accordingly and carry out a Brand MOT after your first year of trading.

 Your annual Brand MOT. Every year give your business a Brand MOT so you can see how well you are progressing in working towards and upholding the vision you have for your business.

- Do your capabilities need re-visiting? If so, which?
- Have things changed in the market? If so, what?
- Has technology moved on? What impact will this have on you?
- Are you sure you are completely satisfying your customers needs?
- Who are your competitors now?
- Are they the same as before?
- Are there any 'new kids on the block'? If so, check them out.
- What are they offering that you are not?
- How do they deal with their customers?
- What are your competitors' pricing strategies?
- How can you make your offer more distinctive/different/better than theirs?

Review your Branding Checklist

Based on your Branding Checklist, check your brand essence, positioning and promise – do these need revision? You can use the exercises at the beginning of the book again to see if they do.

If you think your business vision has changed, re-do the exercises in this book to keep your brand moving forward.

Evaluate your Brand Promise.

How will you gain evidence that you are delivering your Brand Promise?

Big brands use 'mystery shoppers' to test the quality and consistency of their brand experience, and you can employ similar tactics. Ask your family, friends and colleagues to act as mystery shoppers. How do they find your service including ordering procedures, communications, after-sales queries etc.

Make sure you are targeting the right customers and offering them the benefits they want. Carry out research continually. Be creative with your research. Use your web site and your blog (if you have one) to the maximum to gain insight into what your customers think about you and your offer. Google your own business to see what other websites are saying about you.

Combat strength sappers. Get out of that rut! Sometimes we develop something new in a business which we later find is causing problems for our staff, or is too difficult to implement. Deal with it. Adapt, change or delete it. Don't keep on doing it because you developed it. Accept that not all of your ideas are good ones. That's human nature.

Deal with any motivational issues. These can be the downfall of your brand. Are your staff happy with you, with the company culture, with the products and services and with their working practices? If not, find out why and fix it.

Carry out a SWOT analysis again. Analyse your strengths, weaknesses (internally), and your untapped opportunities and threats to your brand (externally). What's holding you back? Don't forget the idea is to change the negative points into positive ones. How will you do this? Uncover again your hidden value – have conviction and confidence.

Develop the way forward and keep focused. You may find that keeping an action plan pinned to the wall or regularly meeting with a mentor really helps you to stay focused. Remember to keep it **SMART.**

Another way of keeping focused is to keep you eye on your favourite brands. These brands can be a source of inspiration and keep you on track. At The Branding Workshop, one of our branding heros is Interbrand so we like reading its web site www.brandchannel.com.

Re-visiting the Animal within

 Back in Section 2 (page 39) we asked you to think about which animal would represent you/your brand. This metaphor can now be extended to give you some insight into your vision of the future.

What animal will you become in 5 years? The same animal as you are now, or a different one?

What will you eat? How will you hunt?

What is your environment like?

How big is your territory?

What will you look like?

How will you feel?

How will you communicate?

Pull out the key points. You may find they communicate some of the values and skills you noted earlier or that they really strike a chord with how you are thinking about your business now, or in the future. This work really gives you more insight into the vision or core idea of your brand.

Competitors

The same method can be a great way to analyse your competitors – what animals are they? What environments are they working in, how do they behave etc? It's good to think of them in this way as it instantly brings to mind a number of characteristics. At the end of your analysis, write down both positive and negative elements about your competitors, things you can improve upon, things you can do better.

Remember also that your competitors aren't always competitors they can also be collaborators, so also note down those you could develop a mutual relationship with.

Market research: remember that this is an essential ongoing activity. Look back at the suggestions in Section 5 (page 102)

 Do you know who your customers really are? When was the last time you really spoke to them? How do you know what they feel about your brand? Is your tattoo in their mind strong, medium or fading?

Think about the following:

- What do you currently have to offer your existing customers that they don't know about?
- When did you last let them know about your new developments?
- What are you not offering existing customers that you could be offering them?
- When did you last send a letter to your customers?
- When did you last email them?
- Did you measure the response?
- When did you last call them?
- What would happen if you doubled your contact with them this year?

When you do communicate with them, what more could you be doing to clearly explain the specific benefits that they will experience from your business?

Once you have thought about these questions, think about some simple ways you could communicate more with them. How about a breakfast shopping sale with croissants and coffee offered to your most loyal customers and there you could introduce privileged shopping events or a simple loyalty scheme.

Perhaps a simple newsletter telling them all what's new about your business activities would be more appropriate (depending on what type of business you have and the number of customers you have).

When thinking about the future of your business, don't forget to keep ahead of trends and new technologies that may change the way you work in 5 years time. It's extremely important to keep abreast of the future as well as the here-and-now.

This is sometimes difficult for small businesses to do, because they have so many other things to do on a day-to-day basis. There are many websites which offer insights on trends, set up an email alert or an RSS feed with them to keep up-to-date painlessly. Check also on your industry's key web sites, what changes are they foreseeing. Make sure you know what's happening in your market tomorrow!

 Make a list of websites, publications and places you already know of that provide this kind of information about your industry. Google them, and notice what else comes up, including the adverts. Who's trying to attract your attention? Add them to your watch list and check them regularly.

Behaviours

The Branding Workshop has worked with over 5000 businesses and we have discovered that those that have grown their brands effectively behave in particular ways.

7 Habits of Highly Effective Small Brands

Let us look at some proven habits of successful small brands:

1. They have vision, focus and leadership. They understand themselves.
2. They dominate their niche, however small.
3. They understand their customers. They are customer-centric.
4. They have a distinctive offer.
5. They are highly creative in marketing.
6. They have credibility.
7. They form emotional connections with their customers.

Let's examine these in a bit more detail, because they are vital for you and your small business to understand.

Habit 1: They have vision, focus and leadership, they understand themselves

Knowing who you are means knowing what you stand for and the culture you want for your brand. These things will govern your communication style (written, oral or visual) and will bring cohesion to the way you develop your business.

What makes you stand out from the rest? What's it like to do business with you? In a nutshell, a brand is a promise of consistency delivered throughout all your communications. This is where your brand culture comes in to play.

To deliver this consistency there has to be a structure and a culture that everyone in your company (or your suppliers and manufacturers) buys into and agrees to. It has to be delivered from the top to the bottom, in both the internal and external environments. If it's just you, the buck stops there, but as soon as you start employing people you then have the task of communicating your vision and focus to them by the way you lead: the way the telephone is answered, the music your clients listen to while on hold, the quality of the company brochure, the articles you write on blogs, and so on. It is this repetitive, consistent delivery of information and communication that defines your company's culture and promotes your core values.

Habit 2: They dominate their niche, however small.

You can't hope to dominate a large sector as a small business, but you can often find a niche where you can make your mark. Being a big fish in a small pond enhances your visibility and credibility. You can attract attention to yourself by being noticed and building your reputation in this area.

Developing niche audiences is a great way to grow a small business. We say that growing a brand niche-by-niche is like eating an elephant - one bite at a time! A contact tree is a great way to start. Start with those contacts you know first, and then make them grow bigger and bigger and bigger!

Habit 3: They understand their customers. They are customer-centric

When you build a brand you have to be customer-centric. Your customer must be at the heart of everything you do. Brands are built in the minds of customers by using all their senses. So, if you make a food product, not only has the taste got to be fantastic, but also the packaging has to display qualities your customer will recognise and respond to.

To do this you have to really research and understand what will turn on your particular customers. Here's how to start.

Create a Customer Universe: write down (or preferably create an A2-sized collage using newspaper and magazine cuttings) your answers to the following questions:

- Who are your target customers?
- What do they look like?
- What is their lifestyle like?
- Who are their children (if they have them)?
- Where do they live?
- Where do they shop and what do they buy?
- Where do they go on holiday?
- What language do they use?
- What other key products would you imagine them buying?
- What marketing language is associated with these key products?

Habit 4: They have a distinctive offer

Ask yourself what's the difference that makes the difference about what I'm bringing to my customers? When you build a brand, your customer must be at the heart of everything you do. Your customers will create internal perceptions about the value your brand brings to them. You need to know what that value is and how you differ from your competitors.

How well do you communicate what you do? Sometimes we only have a matter of seconds to make a good first impression or to explain what we do using differentiation. So if you are making hand-made shoes what's different about yours to the other hand-made shoe sellers in your town or region?

"Talking the Talk" i.e. saying what you mean, is the most cost effective way to market your business. How would you explain what you do in 30 seconds in order to make it understood what makes the difference about the way you do things?

Lifting your pitch. If you met someone in a lift and you had to tell them what you or your company did by the time they left the lift, what would you say? This often happens, we meet someone who could be a potential client or customer, they ask us what we do, and we stammer and spend ages trying to explain.

Your pitch needs to be short and succinct, they used to say 30 seconds was long enough to explain what you do: now, it seems like that is too long, as the listener probably won't remember 30 seconds worth. So you need to make it SMART - Short, Memorable, Appealing, Repeatable, and Timely; a one-liner or headline that our targets will use to recommend us. A catchphrase headline then becomes the predominant theme, tying together all of your marketing communications.

The Branding Workshop's is 'It's not just about logos'. Creativité Consultants is 'Where Creativity Comes from the Heart'. What's yours? Write your pitch here...be as succinct as possible, so that the next time you have 30 seconds to impress someone, you will!

Habit 5: They are highly creative in marketing

When you build a brand your marketing needs to be at the cutting edge. You have to understand which methods will be most effective in attracting your customers.

Great marketing does not have to be expensive, but it has to be imaginative. You have to know how to switch on your marketplace. So if you produce visually exciting products you need to market them with great photos. If you make tasty food, then let the customer sample it.

Habit 6: They have credibility

When you build a brand, your offer in the marketplace needs to be credible. Brands develop by forming trustworthy associations with customers. Saying what you mean and meaning what you say gives you credibility! You must demonstrate trust in all your interactions with the client. If you position yourself as being an expert in something, then that expertise must be demonstrated in everything you do and say.

Habit 7: They form emotional connections with their customers

When you build a brand, you also need to be very close to your customers. You have to personalise your ways of dealing with them. Brands build quickly by forming emotional associations with customers, and if you are genuine with them, you will build strong relationships that then tie them into your world. Customers all like to be treated as individuals, so make sure you remember their names, their children's names and their preferences, and don't forget their birthdays!

Summary

In this section you've seen

- How to set SMART targets
- How to review and/or MOT your brand
- 7 habits of effective brands

It's nearly time for us to leave you, so just one last word before we go...

Conclusion ●●●

You have now seen that the difference that makes the difference is YOU! Over the course of this book you have seen that by using your personality to make your offering unique you develop a magnetic brand that will pull customers towards it. By making branding a conscious activity, you can use credibility and visibility to build your reputation by using your "PVC" to make your offering unique.

But don't just listen to what we have to say about how this book can make a difference, read what made the difference with some of our clients.

"I can honestly say that we would not have been able to create this impact without you all and in such a short time too. We don't now just sell the product, we sell the brand."
www.frutina.com

"We realised that all areas of our business needed to reflect the premium nature of our work, so that we could attract more repeat business. The Branding Workshop has helped us to address this and reposition our offer. We are thrilled at the response of clients to our new marketing campaign."
www.partridgeevents.co.uk

"When we found the Branding Workshop we knew we had just what we required, a straight forward no nonsense experienced business which could take us through a complex process that so many dress up and seriously overcharge for. We enjoyed our workshops with Yvonne, got where we needed to be quickly, effectively and received very good value for the money spent."
Richard Pullen, Managing Partner, www.austinsmithlord.com

Have Courage

Business is not for the faint hearted especially in tougher times. As we mentioned at the start of this book, when the going gets tough, the tough get branding! Now is the time to muster your resources: courage is required in business.

To run a successful brand-led business you need to:

- Be creative
- Motivate others
- Show your leadership ability
- Seek help you might now need

Help is always at hand...we have given you lots of tools to help you, now you need to use them and get stuck in.

There is a world of resources out there and you can be in touch with us through www.thebrandingworkshop.com or our Facebook page where you can sign up to our newsletter or drop us an email. You are not alone!

Remember that old joke? 5 frogs sitting on a log, one decides to jump off how many are left? 5! Because deciding doesn't mean you will do something. Unless there is movement there's no commitment.

Challenge is needed so get out and blow your own trumpet. Be a force for change, a leader not just a reactor. Be part of the bigger picture, locally, regionally, nationally and internationally – with the internet, local suddenly becomes global!

Confidence and courage

Confidence is a key element in building a business - if you are confident you can do anything. If you can do anything you will be confident. Your ability to know yourself and what makes you feel at ease and confident is a huge asset to you in business.

You'll need to be able to cope with all that will be thrown at you in business. Confidence will help you cope so much better. So, develop a positive frame of mind, be courageous and you will not be afraid of taking risks.

 This is your Life. Do you remember this TV show? Have you ever thought how your life would be presented?

We often ask our clients how they will know when they are successful. One way of doing this is to imagine an occasion later in your life where you and your achievements are being celebrated. This might be an awards ceremony, your retirement, an anniversary or even a memorial after you've gone.

What would people be saying about you? How would they remember you? What have you achieved? Let this thinking form the blueprint for how you organise your future. If what you currently imagine is not what you want them to think, you will need to start doing things differently.

So what will you do and how will you do it? What will be your measure of success? When you know this, you will naturally start to achieve it. You can then set an internal compass for our future.

Firstly, jot down your thoughts about your celebration in a list on the right hand side of the box below or on a large sheet of paper. These thoughts should be how you imagine those people who know you will remember you.

Then on the left hand side against each of the "celebration" comments, re-imagine your future by thinking about the things you would like to change, in order to change others' perceptions of you in the future.

Or you can make a new collage of your thinking. Use images and words that demonstrate what you have found out from this exercise. Compare it with your first one. What new thinking has this book brought you?

Once you have done the exercise ask your work colleagues and friends how they would really remember you and compare your notes.

Had a great idea	Creative
Took a risk	Courageous
Built great teams	Empowered others

You now understand what branding is and why it's useful to any business. You have looked at YOU and what you want from your business. You have translated that information into the basis of your brand. You have looked at how to apply that to your business, and how to put it all into practice!

 Your final exercise: Commit Yourself! Before you finish reading this book, we want you to do the last exercise. Commit 3 things to paper NOW! What are you going to do next to make your brand-led business really take off.

I commit to doing these 3 things:

1...

2...

3...

Next, choose the most important one and tell someone you are going to do it. Who are you going to tell?

Now it's up to you to get out and communicate your PVC convincingly and effectively. Enjoy your business journey. You never know YOU could be the next Innocent, Google or Armani, they were all small businesses once!

Please keep in touch with us – we'd love to hear your success stories at www.thebrandingworkshop.com

Good luck! Be GREAT, be the BEST YOU CAN BE and most importantly BE DIFFERENT!

We wish you every success.

Yvonne and Sue

Appendix 1 ●●●

Interpreting your Animal Within

Did you notice any similarities between you and the animal?

What the animal looks like tells you about the personality and outward appearance of your brand.

Its behaviour patterns could give you more clarity about your values.

The environment it lives in talks more about your cultural values.

Its ability to find food tells you about resourcefulness and how good you are at creating business opportunities.

How it communicates can tell you a lot about your communication style including your tone of voice.

Glossary ●●●

Brand culture   the way the brand lives, works and is experienced by the consumer and the employees of the company

Brand essence   distillation of the key personality, value and culture aspects of your brand

Brand personality   any oral communication, rituals, specific personality traits your brand carries

Brand positioning   "the difference that makes the difference" using the Four P's of marketing and your own PVC. The Four Ps, known as The Marketing Mix relates to 'price', 'promotion', 'product', and 'place'. However, in recent times, the 'four Ps' have been expanded to the 'seven Ps' with the addition of 'process (for services)', 'planet' (ecological issues) and 'people'

Brand promise   the promise you will consistently make to your customers *and staff*

Brand reputation   the reputation your brand builds over time with all of its stakeholders

Brand values   the key values *and beliefs* which underpin your brand and normally determine the way it behaves and the things it is passionate about. It can also attract other brands with similar values to form brand partnerships or alliances

Brandstories   anecdotes, stories, tales, references you can use around your brand or its specific products or services to tell to your customers and other stakeholders to bring your brand to life

Customer Relationship Management (CRM)   an all encompassing strategy for managing your company's interactions with its customers, clients and sales prospects. It involves the use of technology to organize, automate, and synchronize principally sales activities, but also those for marketing, customer service, and technical support.

Intellectual Property (IP)   a way of defining, and therefore protecting, your creation or invention

On-line and Off-line channels	On-line channels are those relationships formed through your actions on the internet whether that be via your blog, your web-site or social networks. Off-line speaks of the more traditional channels of marketing through face-to-face interactions and networking, printed promotional materials, print advertising, PR etc.
Permission marketing	emails sent without permission are called SPAM. When you create a list, always include a link where readers can unsubscribe if they want to
Relationship marketing	forming close relationships with your customers to develop longer term relationships (now becoming stronger through social media channels). Relationship marketing differs from other forms of marketing in that it recognizes the long term value of customer relationships and extends communication beyond intrusive advertising and sales promotional messages
Search Engine Optimisation (SEO)	making sure your website is visible to search engines like Google for the key terms that define your business
Small Business	privately owned sole trader or family business
Small or Medium Enterprise (SME)	anything from a sole trader up to 50 employees
Social Media Marketing (SMM)	using social networks like Facebook and Twitter to develop relationships with customers
Tag line	a short sentence which encapsulates the uniqueness of your brand (usually formed from the basis of your brand essence) *(also known as a strapline, or selling line)*
Touchpoints	wherever a customer comes into contact with your brand and its communications
Walk your talk	do what you say you do. (Does what is says on the tin!)

Resources ●●●

Our Websites

The Branding Workshop	www.thebrandingworkshop.com
Creativite Consultants	www.creativiteconsultants.com

Twitter

Yvonne Fuchs	@brandinworkshop
Sue Alouche	@suealouche

Other Websites

Branding	www.brandchannel.com
Brand Extensions	www.thebrandelastic.com
Harvard Business School	www.hbs.edu
Creative tools	www.mindtools.com
Expert talks	www.ted.com
Trends	www.trendhunter.com

Tools

Online surveys	www.surveymonkey.com
Email newsletters	www.mailchimp.com
Website building	www.wordpress.com
	www.moonfruit.com
PESTEL analysis	www.cipd.co.uk
SWOT analysis	www.businessballs.com
RSS feed	www.whatisrss.com

Books

Covey, Steven	Seven Habits of Highly Effective People
Gobe, Marc	Emotional Branding 2.0
Grant Leboff	Sticky Marketing
Tom Peters	Imagine

Made in the USA
Lexington, KY
14 June 2014